中国探险家

Heroes and Role Models | Non-Fiction Series

Copyright © 2022 by Level Learning, INC. and Washington Yu Ying PCS™
Original and Edited Text Copyright © 2022 by Washington Yu Ying PCS™

All rights reserved. No part of this book in whole or part may be reproduced without written permission from the publisher.

Published by Level Learning, INC.

Content Contributors:
Washington Yu Ying PCS™
Level Learning - Jingyao Qi

Illustrations by: Josh Taira

Leveling classification based on Level Level Learning.
For full description, visit www.levellearning.com

ISBN 978-1-64040-001-6
Simplified Chinese Edition

About Level Learning:
Level Learning provides a literacy focused curriculum specifically designed for K-12 Chinese as a Second Language classrooms. Our program offers 20 levels of specific and detailed objectives, leveled texts and passages, mastery-based online assessment, and analytics to enable data-driven instruction. Level Learning reading curriculum for both literature and informational text emphasize grammar and comprehension skills to help teachers develop confident and independent Chinese language readers. The non-fiction series of books are specifically designed to support our informational text course based on multiple national standards. To learn more about our entire offering, visit www.levellearning.com

About Washington Yu Ying PCS™:
Washington Yu Ying PCS is a Mandarin English dual language immersion International Baccalaureate (IB) World school. Yu Ying's mission is to inspire and prepare young people to create a better world by challenging them to reach their full potential in a nurturing Chinese/English educational environment. Yu Ying's comprehensive IB, dual immersion curriculum equips students with global competencies for success in the real world. As a leader in immersion education, Yu Ying is determined to advance Chinese language programs and global citizenry education by helping other schools create and strengthen their Chinese programs. For more information, email: products@washingtonyuying.org

很久以前，中国有一个探险家，他的名字叫郑和。

郑和带很多人坐船去探险。

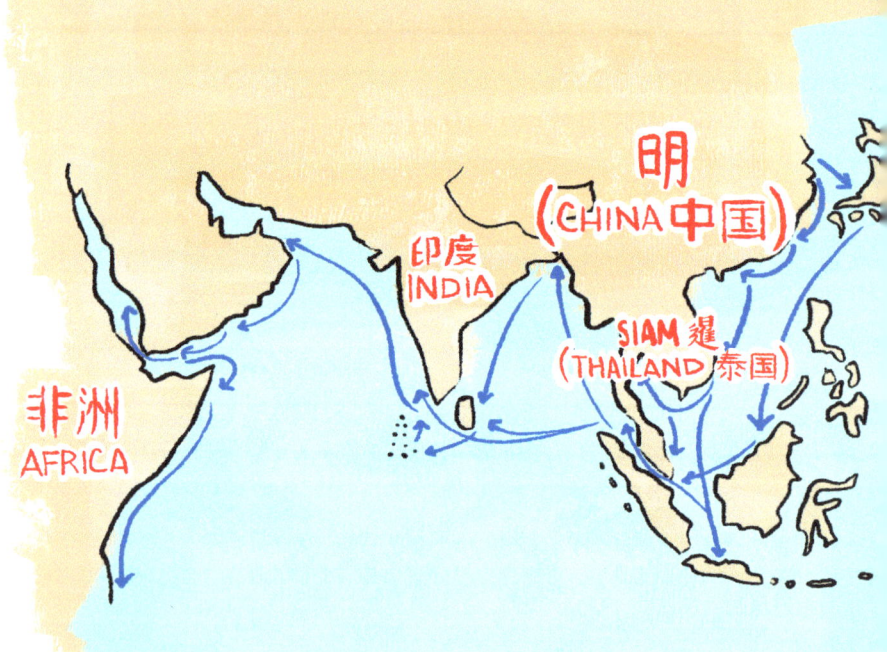

郑和去了外国探险七次。他到了很多地方。

郑和**认识**了很多外国的朋友。

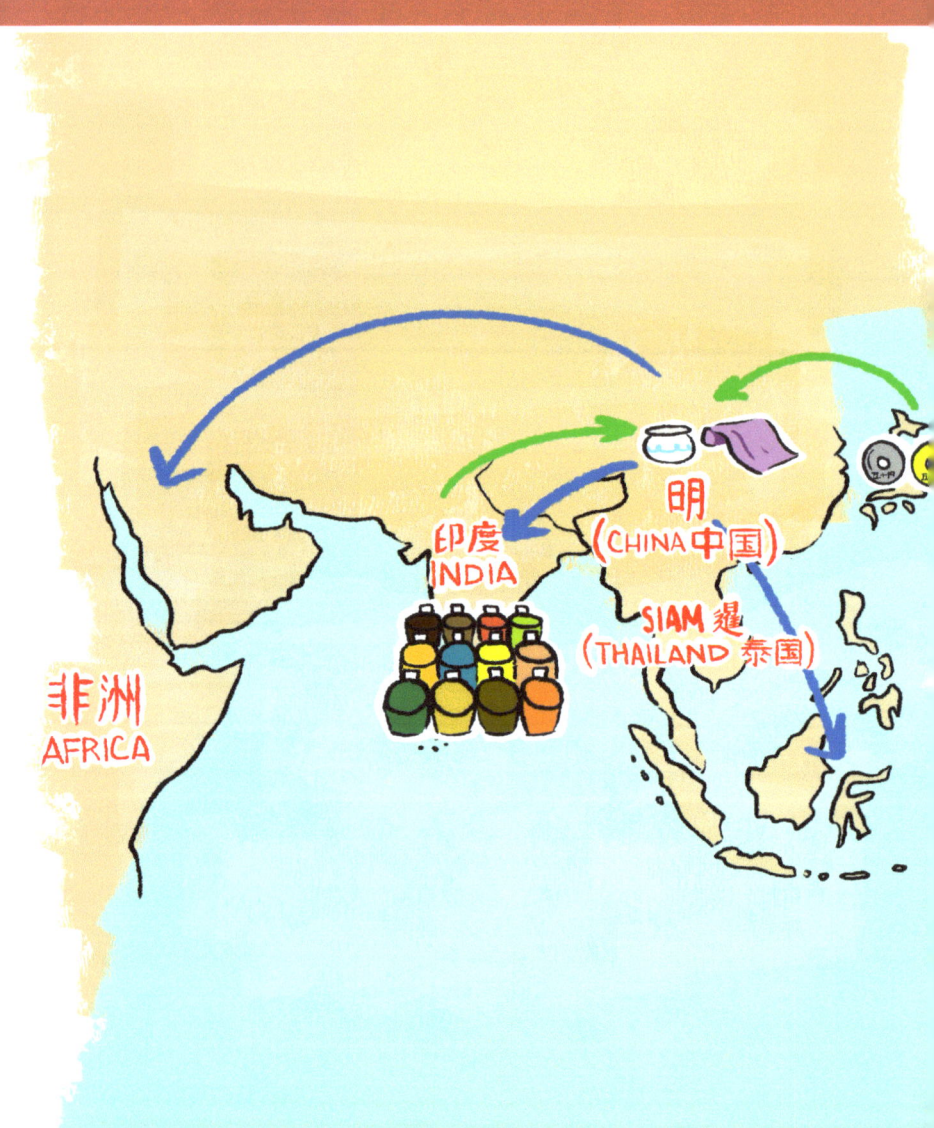

郑和买了很多外国的东西。他也卖了很多中国的东西。

郑和让中国人知道了外国。郑和也让外国人知道了中国。

Glossary

	Pinyin	English Definition
很久以前	hěn jiǔ yǐ qián	long, long ago
探险家	tàn xiǎn jiā	explorer
船	chuán	ship
探险	tàn xiǎn	to explore
外国	wài guó	foreign country
认识	rèn shi	to meet
买	mǎi	to buy
卖	mài	to sell

www.ingramcontent.com/pod-product-compliance
Lightning Source LLC
Chambersburg PA
CBHW041226070526
44584CB00001B/120